IF YOU WANT TO MAKE FRIENDS,
TAKE INITIATIVE! PUT YOURSELF
OUT THERE! HELP AN ESCAPED
CONVICT REMOVE HIS LEG IRON
AND OFFER HIM A PORK PIE!

INSPIRED BY
GREAT EXPECTATIONS, CHARLES DICKENS

FRIENDSHIP IS A TWO-WAY STREET,
NOT A ONE-WAY ROAD. EITHER WAY,
DON'T LET DAISY BUCHANAN DRIVE.

INSPIRED BY
THE GREAT GATSBY, F. SCOTT FITZGERALD

DON'T REFER TO YOURSELF
AND YOUR FRIENDS AS THE
THREE MUSKETEERS IF YOU
HAVEN'T FOILED A NEFARIOUS
PLOT BY CARDINAL RICHELIEU.

INSPIRED BY
THE THREE MUSKETEERS, ALEXANDRE DUMAS

I REALLY RELATE TO BERTHA
MASON. I ALWAYS FELT LIKE
THE TWO OF US WOULD GET
ALONG LIKE A HOUSE ON FIRE.

INSPIRED BY
JANE EYRE, CHARLOTTE BRONTË

TRUE FRIENDSHIP CAN SURVIVE
TIME, DISTANCE, AND THE FACT
THAT ONE OF YOU ACCEPTED
THE MARRIAGE PROPOSAL OF
THE BUMBLING MR. COLLINS.

INSPIRED BY
PRIDE AND PREJUDICE, JANE AUSTEN

A GOOD FRIEND WILL ALWAYS BE THERE FOR YOU. A BEST FRIEND WILL SLAY TYBALT TO AVENGE YOUR DEATH AFTER AN ILL-FATED DUEL IN FAIR VERONA.

INSPIRED BY
ROMEO AND JULIET, WILLIAM SHAKESPEARE

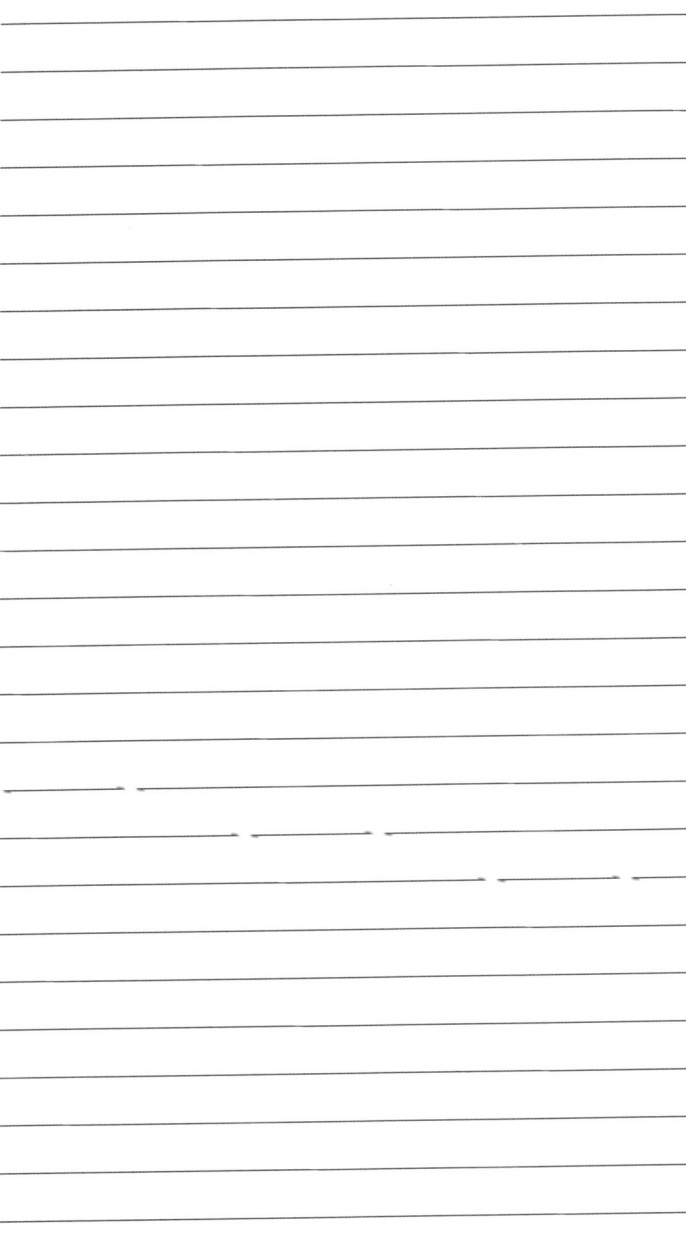

WHAT'S A LITTLE CASK OF
AMONTILLADO BETWEEN FRIENDS?

INSPIRED BY
"THE CASK OF AMONTILLADO," EDGAR ALLAN POE

FRIENDSHIP IS A GIFT, BUT SO WAS
THAT CURSED PORTRAIT IN THE
ATTIC THAT BEARS THE MARKS
OF YOUR SOUL'S CORRUPTION.

INSPIRED BY
THE PICTURE OF DORIAN GRAY, OSCAR WILDE

THE WORST PART ABOUT
MAKING NEW FRIENDS IS WHEN
IT TURNS OUT THEY SLEEP IN
A COFFIN, DRINK BLOOD, CAN
TRANSFORM INTO A BAT, AND
HAVE NO INTENTION OF LETTING
YOU LEAVE CASTLE DRACULA.

INSPIRED BY
DRACULA, BRAM STOKER

LIFE'S TOO SHORT TO BE FRIENDS
WITH PEOPLE WHO WOULD
ASSASSINATE YOU ON THE
WORD OF THREE WITCHES TO
STEAL THE SCOTTISH THRONE.

INSPIRED BY
MACBETH, WILLIAM SHAKESPEARE

MAYBE THE REAL BEAST
IN THE JUNGLE WAS ONE
OF THE FRIENDS WE MADE
ALONG THE WAY.

INSPIRED BY
LORD OF THE FLIES, WILLIAM GOLDING

IF YOU'VE NEVER SOLVED CRIMES
TOGETHER USING LOGIC, FORENSIC
SCIENCE, AND UNPARALLELED
POWERS OF OBSERVATION, ARE
YOU REALLY EVEN FRIENDS?

INSPIRED BY
THE SHERLOCK HOLMES SERIES, ARTHUR CONAN DOYLE

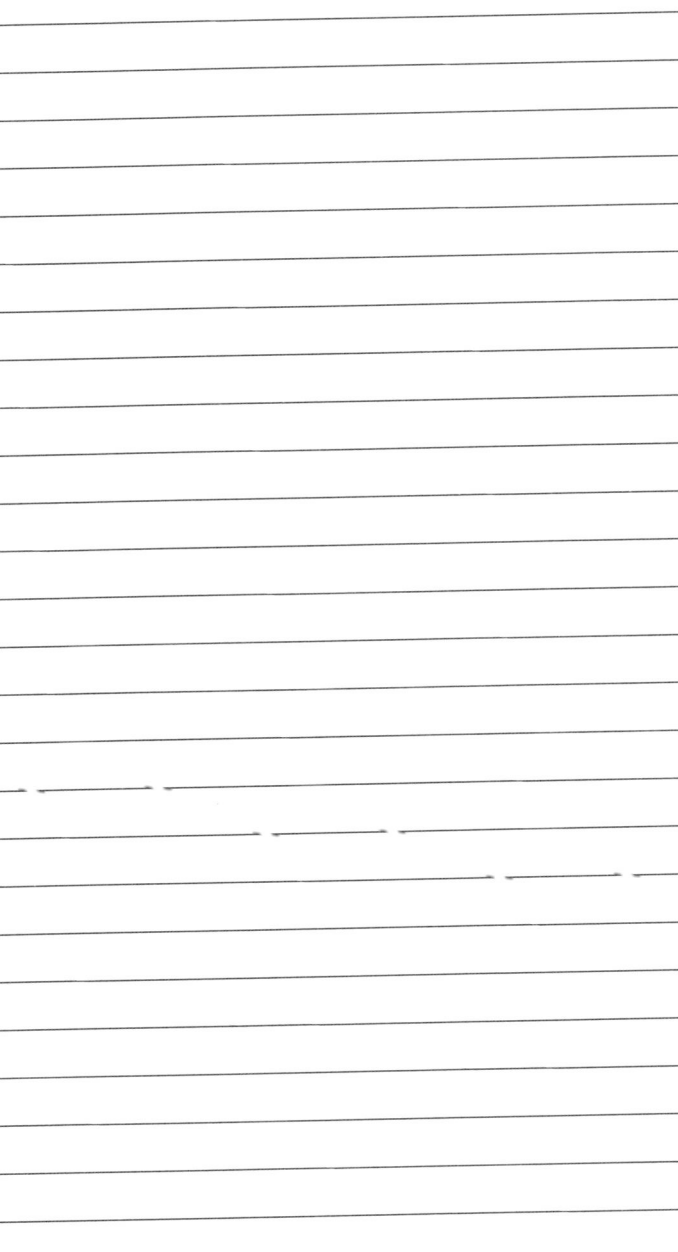

FRIENDSHIP IS LIKE A
FIRST EDITION OF TOLSTOY'S
WAR AND PEACE—IT'S EXTREMELY
VALUABLE AND IT NEVER ENDS.

INSPIRED BY
WAR AND PEACE, LEO TOLSTOY

FAKE FRIENDS WILL TALK BEHIND
YOUR BACK. A REAL FRIEND WILL
SIT WITH YOU ON THE PORCH
AND LISTEN TO YOUR STORY
AFTER YOU RETURN FROM THE
EVERGLADES WITHOUT TEA CAKE.

INSPIRED BY
THEIR EYES WERE WATCHING GOD, ZORA NEALE HURSTON

WHAT ARE FRIENDS FOR? BESIDES
SAYING THINGS LIKE "FRIENDS,
ROMANS, COUNTRYMEN, LEND
ME YOUR EARS; I COME TO BURY
CAESAR, NOT TO PRAISE HIM."

INSPIRED BY
JULIUS CAESAR, WILLIAM SHAKESPEARE

FRIENDSHIP ISN'T ABOUT WHO
YOU'VE KNOWN THE LONGEST.
IT'S ABOUT WHO YOU WANT BY
YOUR SIDE WHEN YOU DIE IN A
DUEL WITH LAERTES AND BRING
THE ENTIRE DANISH ROYAL
FAMILY DOWN WITH YOU.

INSPIRED BY
HAMLET, WILLIAM SHAKESPEARE

FRIENDS DON'T LET FRIENDS GET
SENT TO THE NOTORIOUS FRENCH
PRISON CHATEAU D'IF FOR A
CRIME THEY DIDN'T COMMIT.

INSPIRED BY
THE COUNT OF MONTE CRISTO, ALEXANDRE DUMAS

EVERY FRIEND GROUP HAS A
MAD KING, A TRAGIC HEROINE, A
FOOL, A NOBLEMAN DISGUISED
AS A PEASANT, TWO SISTERS
PLOTTING TO OBTAIN THEIR
FATHER'S KINGDOM THROUGH
FALSE FLATTERY, AND THE
EARL OF GLOUCESTER.

INSPIRED BY
KING LEAR, WILLIAM SHAKESPEARE

STERLING
New York

An Imprint of Sterling Publishing Co., Inc.

STERLING and the distinctive Sterling logo
are registered trademarks of Sterling Publishing Co., Inc.

ISBN 978-1-4549-4490-4

Distributed in Canada by Sterling Publishing Co., Inc.
c/o Canadian Manda Group, 664 Annette Street
Toronto, Ontario, Canada M6S 2C8
Distributed in the United Kingdom by GMC Distribution Services
Castle Place, 166 High Street, Lewes, East Sussex, England BN7 1XU
Distributed in Australia by NewSouth Books
University of New South Wales, Sydney, NSW 2052, Australia

For information about custom editions, special sales,
and premium and corporate purchases, please contact
Sterling Special Sales at 800-805-5489
or specialsales@sterlingpublishing.com.

Manufactured in India

2 4 6 8 10 9 7 5 3 1

sterlingpublishing.com

Text by Courtney Gorter
Design by Christine Heun
Cover by Melissa Farris